The World's Greatest Baseball Players

by Matt Doeden

CAPSTONE PRESS
a capstone imprint

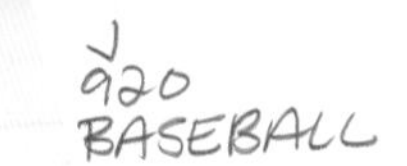

Sports Illustrated KIDS The World's Greatest Sports Stars is published by Capstone Press,
151 Good Counsel Drive, P.O. Box 669, Mankato, Minnesota 56002.
www.capstonepress.com

Printed in the United States of America in Stevens Point, Wisconsin.

092009
005619WZS10

Books published by Capstone Press are manufactured with paper containing at least 10 percent post-consumer waste.

Library of Congress Cataloging-in-Publication Data
Doeden, Matt.
The world's greatest baseball players / by Matt Doeden.
p. cm. — (Sports Illustrated Kids, the world's greatest sports stars)
Includes bibliographical references and index.
Summary: "Describes the achievements and career statistics of baseball's greatest stars" — Provided by publisher.
ISBN 978-1-4296-3922-4 (library binding)
ISBN 978-1-4296-4868-4 (paperback)
1. Baseball players — United States — Biography — Juvenile literature.
I. Title. II. Series.
GV865.A1D64 2010
796.357092'2 — dc22
[B] 2009028534

Editorial Credits
Aaron Sautter, editor; Tracy Davies, designer; Eric Gohl, media researcher; Laura Manthe, production specialist

Photo Credits
MLB Photos via Getty Images/Mark Cunningham, 20
Shutterstock/Ksash, backgrounds
Sports Illustrated/Al Tielemans, 1 (center), 6; Bob Rosato, 28; Chuck Solomon, 1 (left), 4–5 (background), 4 (left), 5 (right), 10, 15, 18, 30–31 (background); Damian Strohmeyer, cover, 17, 27; David E. Klutho, 1 (right), 4 (right), 12; John Iacono, 9, 24; John W. McDonough, 5 (left), 23

Statistics in this book are current through the 2009 MLB season.

Table of Contents

Play Ball!

Crack! Ryan Howard smashes a home run over the fence. Zing! Johan Santana zips a fastball over the plate. Baseball is known as America's pastime. Fans love big home runs, fierce pitching duels, and great defensive plays. They enjoy spending the summer rooting for Major League Baseball's (MLB's) greatest players.

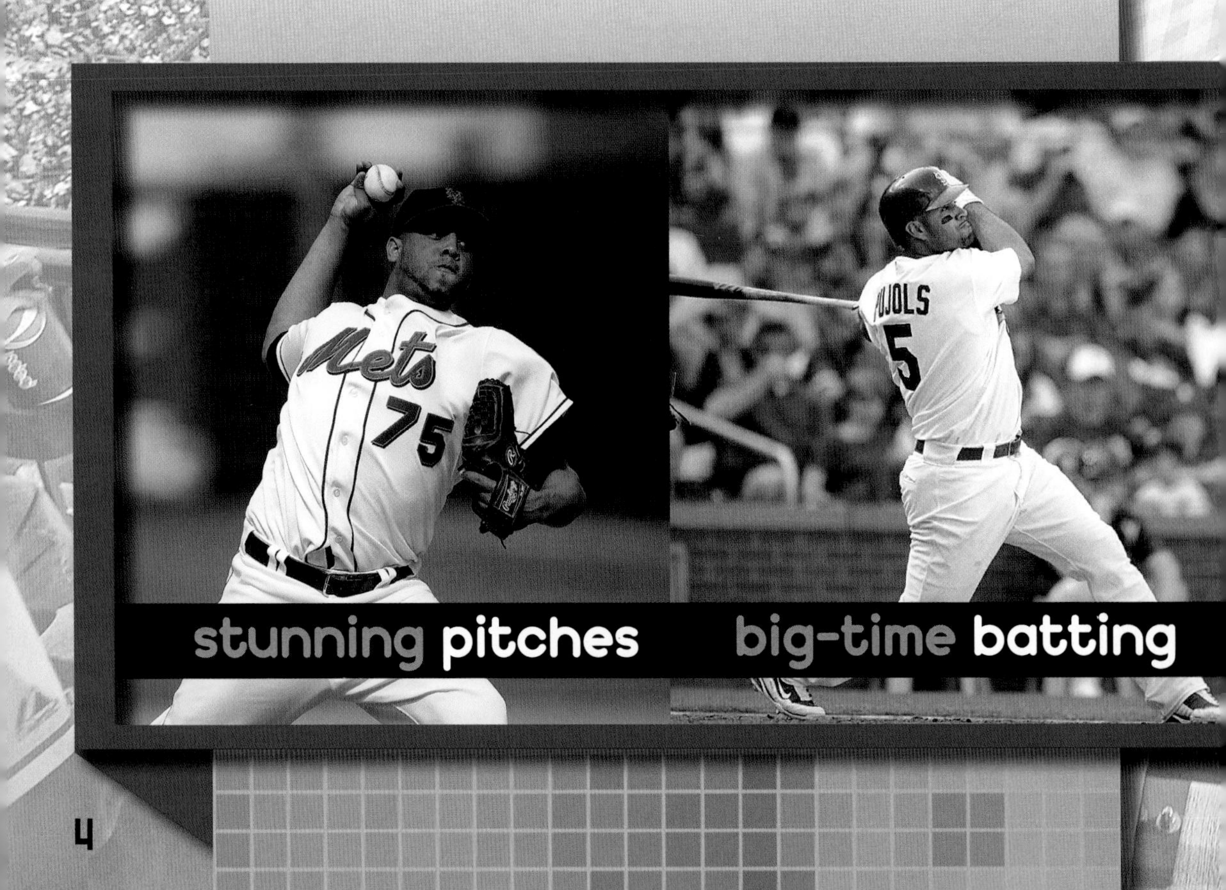

stunning pitches

big-time batting

incredible catches

daring base running

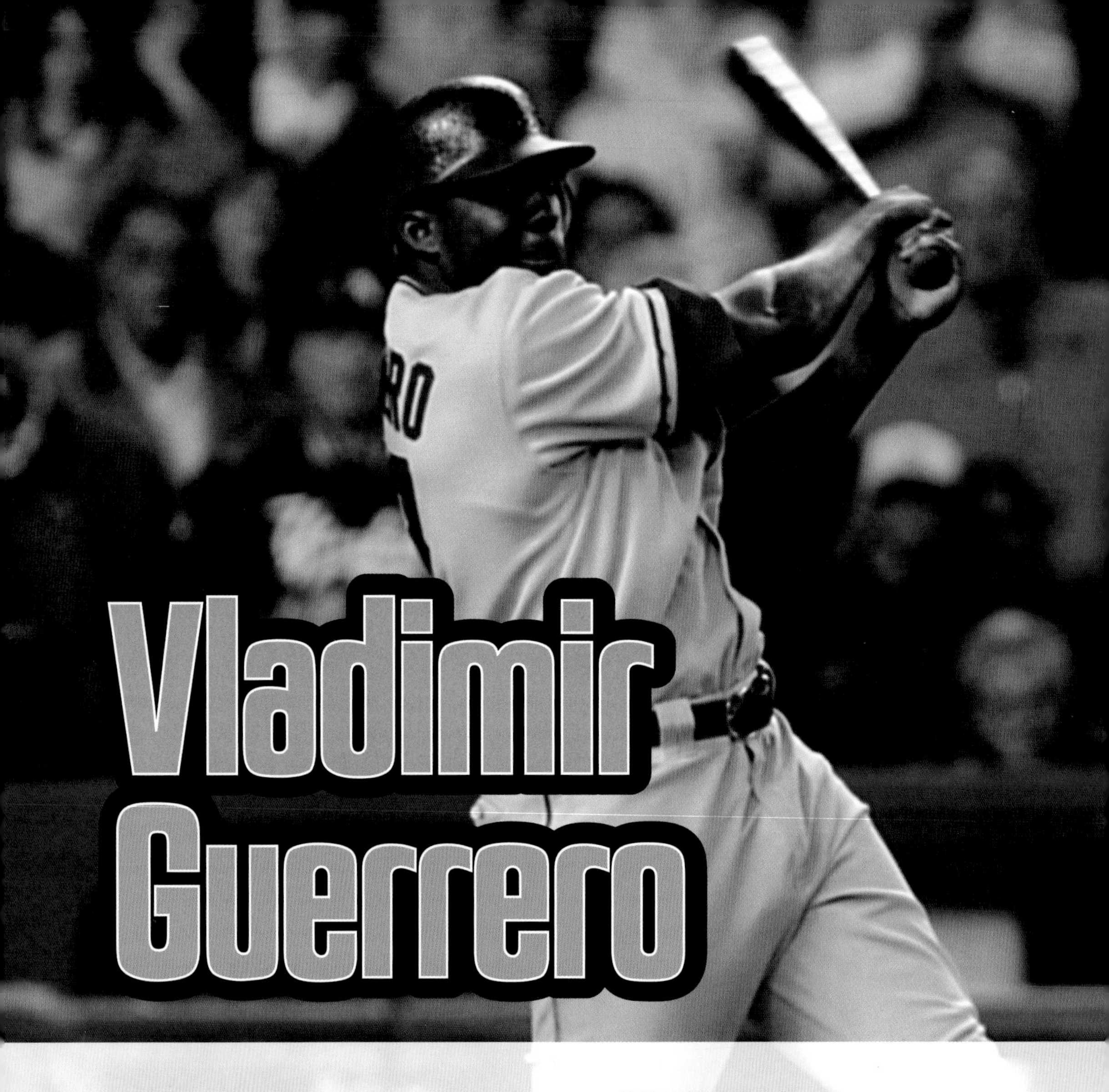

Vladimir Guerrero

It's tough to get a pitch past Vladimir Guerrero. The Los Angeles Angels outfielder is one of the best hitters in baseball. He can hit pitches in the **strike zone** or out of it. Guerrero started his career with the Montreal Expos. He joined the Angels in 2004. He won the American League (AL) Most Valuable Player (MVP) Award that same year. Guerrero has also been an eight-time All-Star.

personal information

Name: Vladimir Alvino Guerrero
Born: February 9, 1975, in Nizao Bani, Dominican Republic
Height: 6 feet, 3 inches
Weight: 235 pounds
Bats: Right Throws: Right Position: Outfield

Regular Season Stats

Year	Team	Games	Hits	HR	RBI	AVG
1996	MON	9	5	1	1	.185
1997	MON	90	98	11	40	.302
1998	MON	159	202	38	109	.324
1999	MON	160	193	42	131	.316
2000	MON	154	197	44	123	.345
2001	MON	159	184	34	108	.307
2002	MON	161	206	39	111	.336
2003	MON	112	130	25	79	.330
2004	ANA	156	206	39	126	.337
2005	LAA	141	165	32	108	.317
2006	LAA	156	200	33	116	.329
2007	LAA	150	186	27	125	.324
2008	LAA	143	164	27	91	.303
2009	LAA	100	113	15	50	.295
CAREER		**1,850**	**2,249**	**407**	**1,318**	**.321**

(HR = Home Runs; RBI = Runs Batted In; AVG = Batting Average)

strike zone: the area above home plate between a batter's knees and shoulders

achievements

All-Star selection: 1999, 2000, 2001, 2002, 2004, 2005, 2006, 2007
American League MVP: 2004
Silver Slugger Award: 1999, 2000, 2002, 2004, 2005, 2006, 2007
Home Run Derby champion: 2007
National League home run leader (44): 2000

fact

Guerrero doesn't like using batting gloves. He says his hands are tough because as a boy, he pulled cows home with his bare hands.

personal information

Name: Derek Sanderson Jeter
Born: June 26, 1974, in Pequannock, New Jersey
Height: 6 feet, 3 inches
Weight: 195 pounds
Bats: Right   Throws: Right   Position: Shortstop

Regular Season Stats

Year	Team	Games	Hits	HR	RBI	AVG
1995	NYY	15	12	0	7	.250
1996	NYY	157	183	10	78	.314
1997	NYY	159	190	10	70	.291
1998	NYY	149	203	19	84	.324
1999	NYY	158	219	24	102	.349
2000	NYY	148	201	15	73	.339
2001	NYY	150	191	21	74	.311
2002	NYY	157	191	18	75	.297
2003	NYY	119	156	10	52	.324
2004	NYY	154	188	23	78	.292
2005	NYY	159	202	19	70	.309
2006	NYY	154	214	14	97	.343
2007	NYY	156	206	12	73	.322
2008	NYY	150	179	11	69	.300
2009	NYY	153	212	18	66	.334
CAREER		**2,138**	**2,747**	**224**	**1,068**	**.317**

(HR = Home Runs; RBI = Runs Batted In; AVG = Batting Average)

achievements

All-Star selection: 1998, 1999, 2000, 2001, 2002, 2004, 2006, 2007, 2008, 2009
American League Rookie of the Year: 1996
World Series MVP: 2000
Gold Glove Award: 2004, 2005, 2006
New York Yankees Player of the Year: 1998, 1999, 2000, 2006

fact

In 2000, Jeter won both the All-Star Game MVP and the World Series MVP. He was the first player ever to win both awards in the same season.

Derek Jeter

The New York Yankees' Derek Jeter is always confident. He has reason to be. Jeter is one of the game's great shortstops. Jeter has been a winner since he began his major league career. In 1996, he won the AL Rookie of the Year Award. Since then, he's been a nine-time All-Star and a four-time World Series champion.

Francisco Rodriguez

At times, the New York Mets' Francisco Rodriguez seems totally unhittable. Batters can only stand and watch as his pitches zip across the plate. Rodriguez's nickname is "K-Rod." The *K* is baseball's symbol for a **strikeout**. Rodriguez's best year was in 2008 with the Los Angeles Angels. He set a major league record with 62 **saves**.

personal information

Name: Francisco José Rodriguez
Born: January 7, 1982, in Caracas, Venezuela
Height: 6 feet
Weight: 195 pounds
Bats: Right   Throws: Right
Position: Relief Pitcher

Regular Season Stats

Year	Team	Games	Wins	Losses	ERA	Saves
2002	ANA	5	0	0	0.00	0
2003	ANA	59	8	3	3.03	2
2004	ANA	69	4	1	1.82	12
2005	LAA	66	2	5	2.67	45
2006	LAA	69	2	3	1.73	47
2007	LAA	64	5	2	2.81	40
2008	LAA	76	2	3	2.24	62
2009	NYM	70	3	6	3.71	35
CAREER		**478**	**26**	**23**	**2.53**	**243**

(ERA = Earned Run Average)

achievements

All-Star selection: 2004, 2007, 2008, 2009
Led American League in saves: 2005, 2006, 2008
Rolaids Relief Man of the Year Award: 2006, 2008
Major league record 62 saves in 2008
World Series champion: 2002

strikeout: when a pitcher throws three strikes against a batter

save: when a relief pitcher helps his team keep a small lead to win a game

fact In 2006, Rodriguez saved his 100th career game at age 24. He became the youngest pitcher ever to reach that mark.

Albert Pujols

Albert Pujols may be the most dangerous hitter playing today. He's never finished a season with a **batting average** lower than .314. He's also smacked at least 32 home runs each season. The two-time National League (NL) MVP led the St. Louis Cardinals to a World Series title in 2006.

personal information

Name: José Alberto Pujols
Born: January 16, 1980, in Santo Domingo, Dominican Republic
Height: 6 feet, 3 inches
Weight: 230 pounds
Bats: Right Throws: Right Position: First Base

Regular Season Stats

Year	Team	Games	Hits	HR	RBI	AVG
2001	STL	161	194	37	130	.329
2002	STL	157	185	34	127	.314
2003	STL	157	212	43	124	.359
2004	STL	154	196	46	123	.331
2005	STL	161	195	41	117	.330
2006	STL	143	177	49	137	.331
2007	STL	158	185	32	103	.327
2008	STL	148	187	37	116	.357
2009	STL	160	186	47	135	.327
CAREER		**1,399**	**1,717**	**366**	**1,112**	**.334**

(HR = Home Runs; RBI = Runs Batted In; AVG = Batting Average)

achievements

All-Star selection: 2001, 2003, 2004, 2005, 2006, 2007, 2008, 2009
National League MVP: 2005, 2008
National League batting champion: 2003
National League Championship Series MVP: 2004
Gold Glove Award: 2006

batting average: a measure of how often a batter gets a base hit

fact

Pujols started his career as an outfielder. He then played third base before becoming the Cardinals' regular first baseman.

personal information

Name: Hanley Ramirez
Born: December 23, 1983, in Samana, Dominican Republic
Height: 6 feet, 3 inches
Weight: 225 pounds
Bats: Right Throws: Right Position: Shortstop

Regular Season Stats

Year	Team	Games	Hits	HR	RBI	AVG
2005	BOS	2	0	0	0	.000
2006	FLA	158	185	17	59	.292
2007	FLA	154	212	29	81	.332
2008	FLA	153	177	33	67	.301
2009	FLA	151	197	24	106	.342
CAREER		**618**	**771**	**103**	**313**	**.316**

(HR = Home Runs; RBI = Runs Batted In; AVG = Batting Average)

achievements

All-Star selection: 2008, 2009
National League Rookie of the Year: 2006
Silver Slugger Award: 2008
Florida Marlins team MVP: 2008

fact In 2008, Ramirez led the league in scoring with 125 runs.

Hanley Ramirez

Hanley Ramirez is an all-around talent. He's a skilled hitter, a fast runner, and plays great defense. In 2006, he hit 17 home runs for the Florida Marlins. He also stole 51 bases. Those numbers earned him the NL Rookie of the Year Award. Ramirez has continued to get even better. He batted for a .332 average in 2007. In 2008, he smacked 33 homers.

personal information

Name: Joseph Patrick Mauer
Born: April 19, 1983, in St. Paul, Minnesota
Height: 6 feet, 5 inches
Weight: 225 pounds
Bats: Left Throws: Right Position: Catcher

Regular Season Stats

Year	Team	Games	Hits	HR	RBI	AVG
2004	MIN	35	33	6	17	.308
2005	MIN	131	144	9	55	.294
2006	MIN	140	181	13	84	.347
2007	MIN	109	119	7	60	.293
2008	MIN	146	176	9	85	.328
2009	MIN	137	189	28	96	.364
CAREER		**698**	**842**	**72**	**397**	**.327**

(HR = Home Runs; RBI = Runs Batted In; AVG = Batting Average)

achievements

All-Star selection: 2006, 2008, 2009
American League batting champion: 2006, 2008
Silver Slugger Award: 2006, 2008
Gold Glove Award: 2008
Number one overall pick of the 2001 amateur draft

fact

Mauer was a star quarterback and an All-American in high school. He was offered a scholarship to play football for Florida State University.

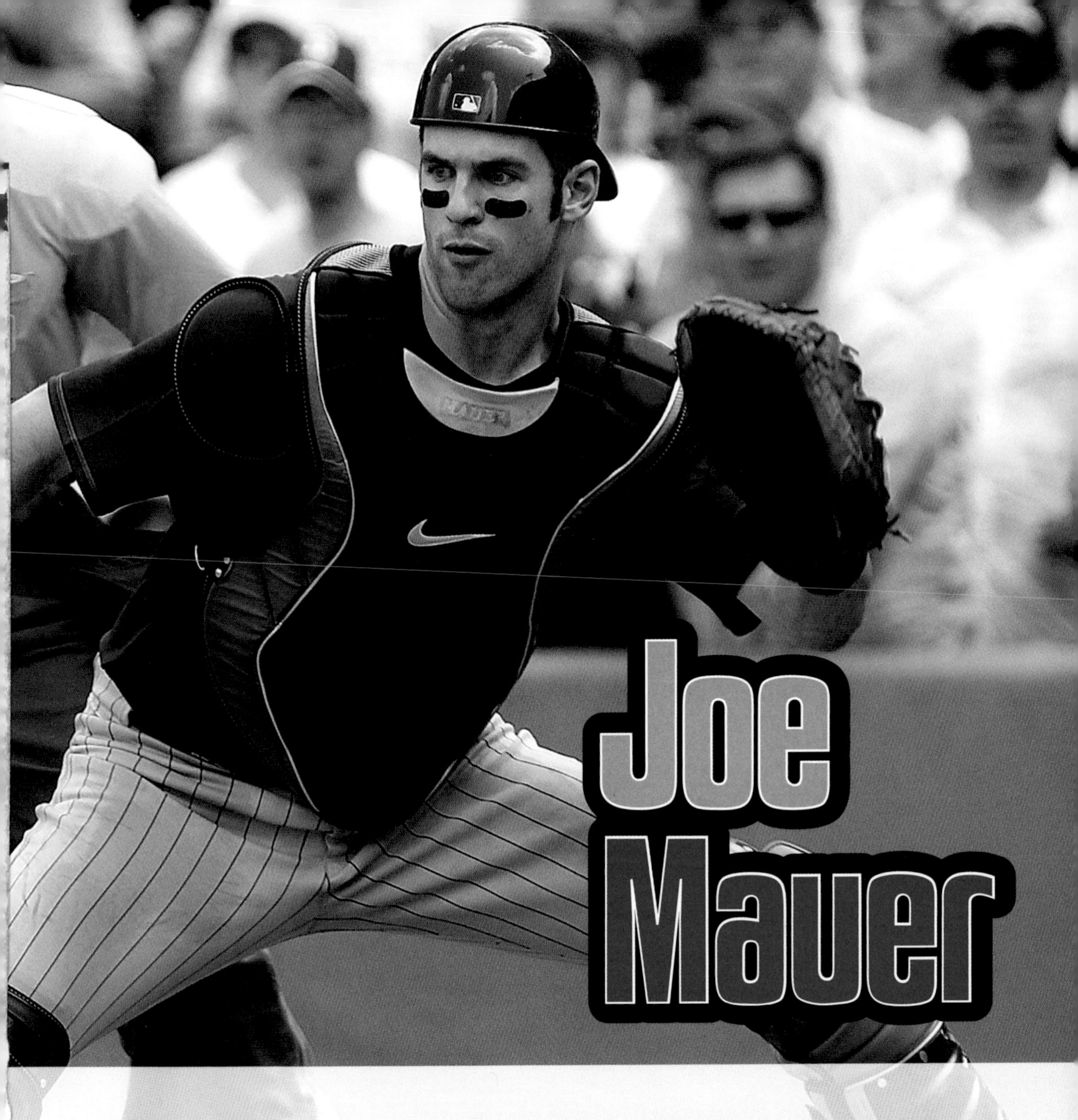

Joe Mauer

Joe Mauer's swing is a thing of beauty. Few hitters are better at waiting for just the right pitch. In 2006, the Minnesota Twins' star became the first American League catcher to win the batting title. He did it again in 2008. Mauer is also a defensive star. Base runners think twice before trying to steal against his rocket arm.

Matt Holliday

When Matt Holliday steps up to the plate, everyone takes notice. The St. Louis Cardinals outfielder bats for a high average and great power. He's also a threat to steal anytime he's on base. In 2007, Holliday helped lead the Colorado Rockies to the World Series. In 2009, he played for the Oakland Athletics before being traded to St. Louis.

personal information

Name: Matthew Thomas Holliday
Born: January 15, 1980, in Stillwater, Oklahoma
Height: 6 feet, 4 inches
Weight: 235 pounds
Bats: Right Throws: Right Position: Outfield

Regular Season Stats

Year	Team	Games	Hits	HR	RBI	AVG
2004	COL	121	116	14	57	.290
2005	COL	125	147	19	87	.307
2006	COL	155	196	34	114	.326
2007	COL	158	216	36	137	.340
2008	COL	139	173	25	88	.321
2009	OAK/STL	156	182	24	109	.313
CAREER		**854**	**1,030**	**152**	**592**	**.318**

(HR = Home Runs; RBI = Runs Batted In; AVG = Batting Average)

achievements

All-Star selection: 2006, 2007, 2008
Silver Slugger Award: 2006, 2007, 2008
National League batting champion: 2007
2007 National League Championship Series MVP
Baseball America All-Rookie Team: 2004

fact

Holliday played quarterback in high school. He was offered a scholarship to play football for Oklahoma State University.

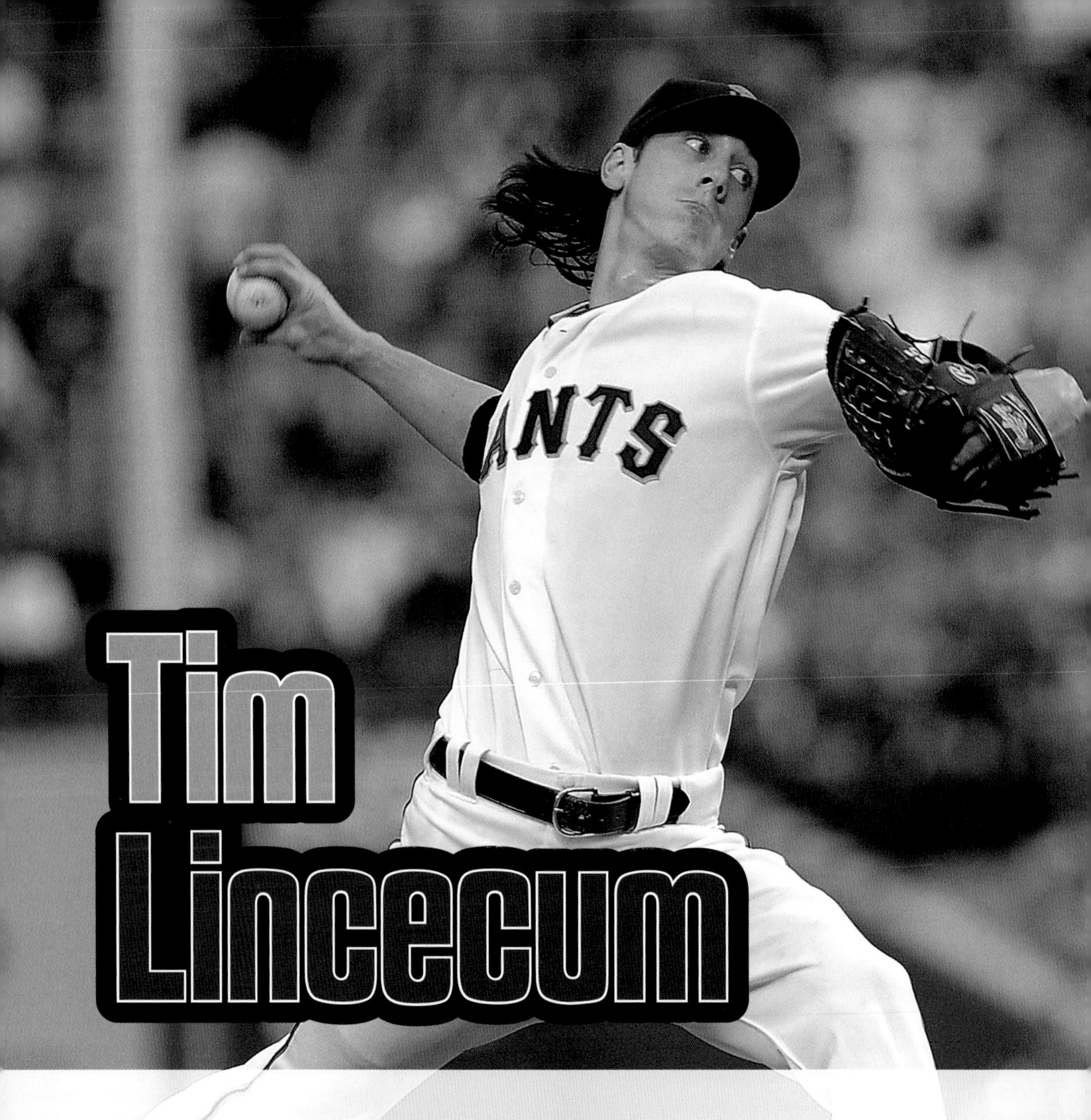

Tim Lincecum

Tim Lincecum doesn't look like a major threat on the field. The San Francisco Giants' hurler isn't as tall or heavy as most power pitchers. But his fastball clocks in at 95 miles per hour or faster. He also has a great curveball and **changeup**. His amazing pitching skills earned him the NL Cy Young Award in 2008.

personal information

Name: Timothy Leroy Lincecum
Born: June 15, 1984, in Bellevue, Washington
Height: 5 feet, 11 inches
Weight: 170 pounds
Bats: Left Throws: Right
Position: Starting Pitcher

Regular Season Stats

Year	Team	Games	Wins	Losses	Strikeouts	ERA
2007	SFG	24	7	5	150	4.00
2008	SFG	34	18	5	265	2.62
2009	SFG	32	15	7	261	2.48
CAREER		**90**	**40**	**17**	**676**	**2.90**

(ERA = Earned Run Average)

achievements

All-Star selection: 2008, 2009
National League Cy Young Award: 2008
Led National League in strikeouts (265) in 2008
Golden Spikes Award (given to best amateur baseball player): 2006

changeup: a pitch that looks like a fastball but is actually much slower

fact

Despite his wild delivery, Lincecum is accurate in his throws. His father taught him the unusual pitching style to pack more power behind his pitch.

personal information

Name: Dustin Luis Pedroia
Born: August 17, 1983, in Woodland, California
Height: 5 feet, 9 inches
Weight: 180 pounds
Bats: Right Throws: Right
Position: Second Base

Regular Season Stats

Year	Team	Games	Hits	HR	RBI	AVG
2006	BOS	31	17	2	7	.191
2007	BOS	139	165	8	50	.317
2008	BOS	157	213	17	83	.326
2009	BOS	154	185	15	72	.296
CAREER		**481**	**580**	**42**	**212**	**.307**

(HR = Home Runs; RBI = Runs Batted In; AVG = Batting Average)

achievements

All-Star selection: 2008, 2009
American League Rookie of the Year: 2007
American League MVP: 2008
Gold Glove Award: 2008
Silver Slugger Award: 2008

fact In the 2007 World Series, Pedroia became the first rookie to lead off game one with a home run.

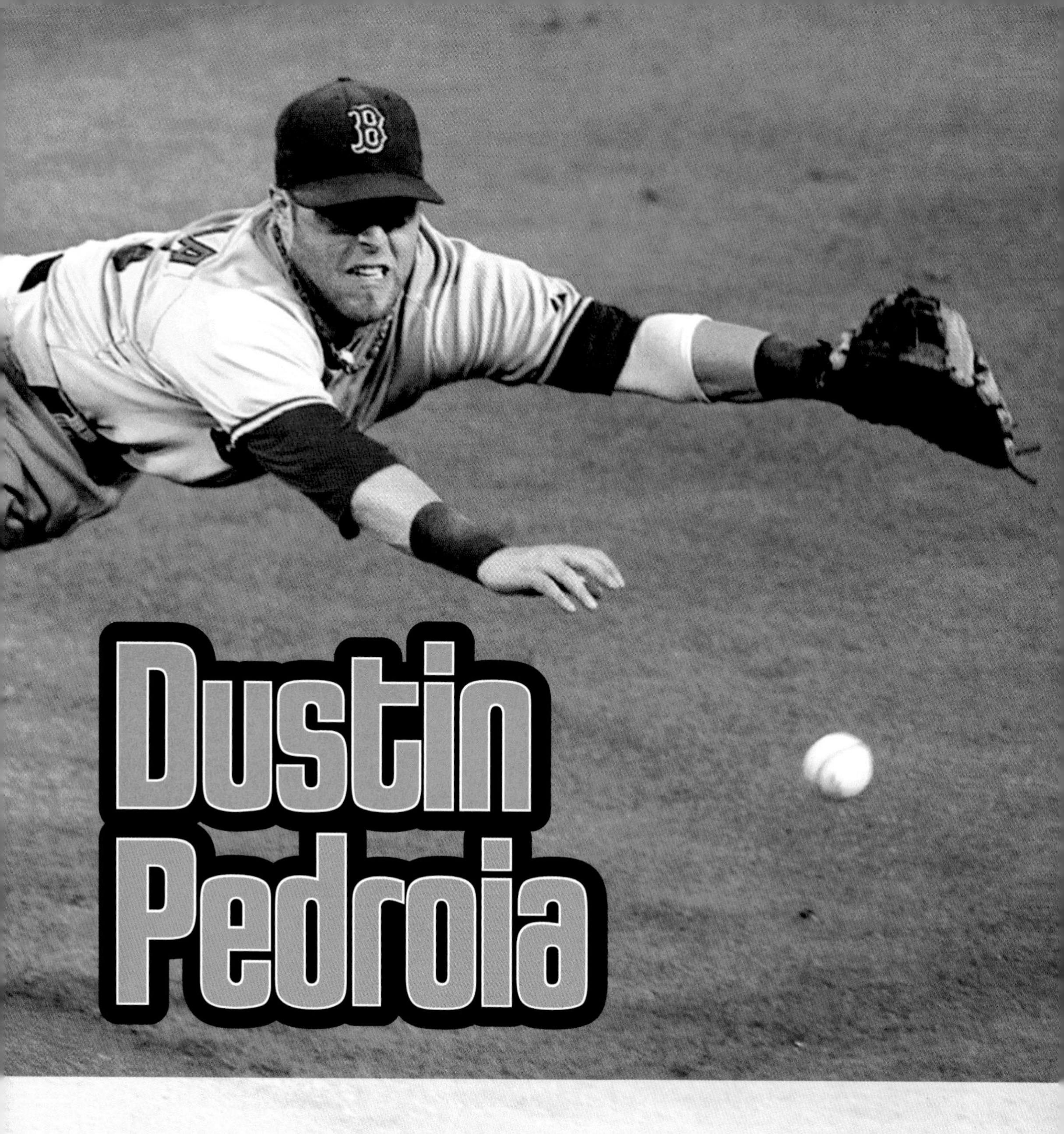

Dustin Pedroia

Dustin Pedroia spends a lot of time in the dirt. He dives all around the infield. He slides into bases at full speed. Pedroia's scrappy play helped him win the AL Rookie of the Year Award in 2007. He also helped the Boston Red Sox win the World Series that year. Then in 2008, he won the AL MVP trophy.

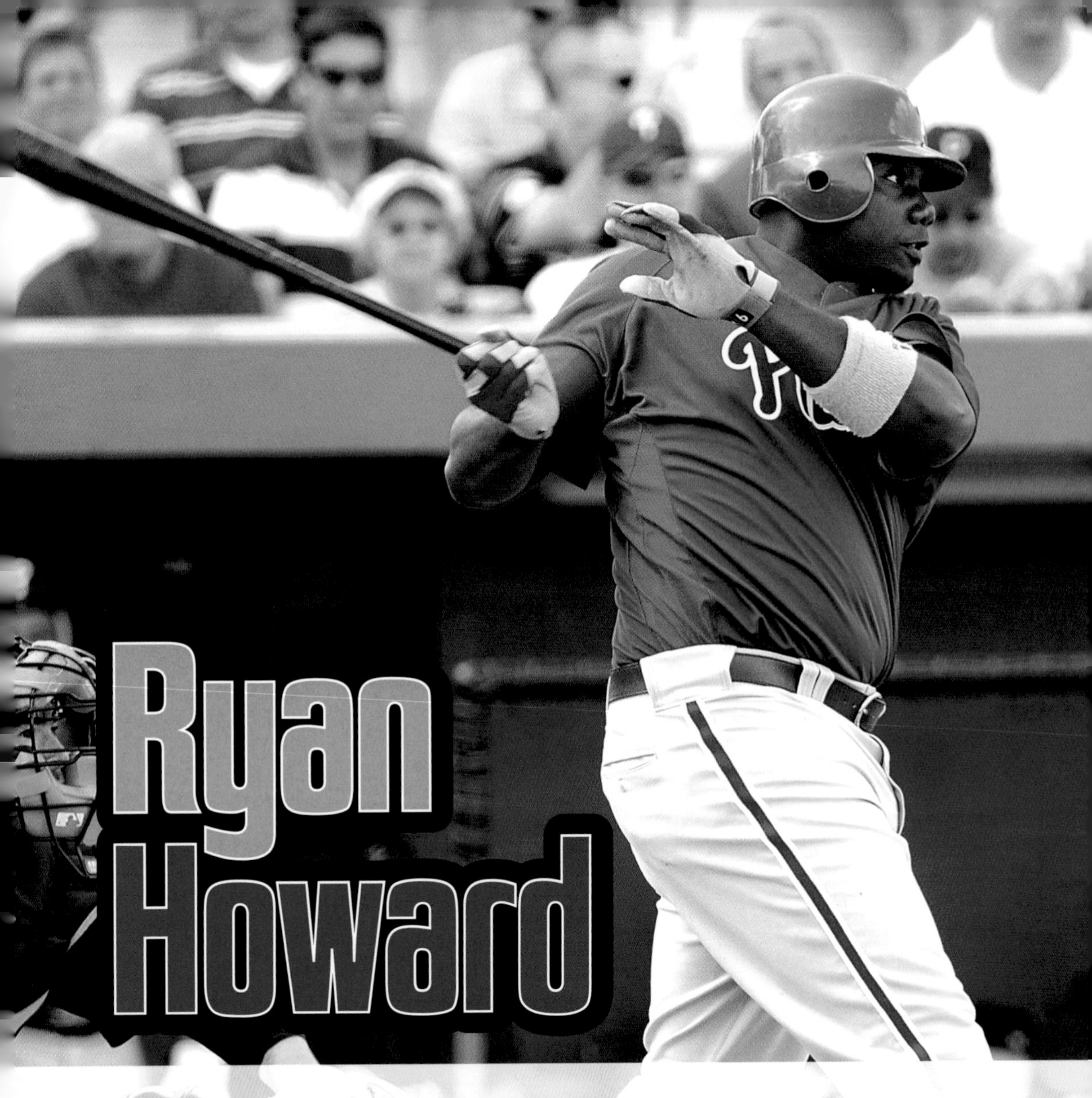

Ryan Howard

Ryan Howard can flat-out crush a baseball. In 2006, the young slugger smashed 58 home runs during his first full season. He also batted a .313 average. He was an easy pick for the 2006 NL MVP. Howard was even better in the 2008 World Series. He hit three homers to help the Philadelphia Phillies win the championship.

Name: Ryan James Howard
Born: November 19, 1979, in St. Louis, Missouri
Height: 6 feet, 4 inches
Weight: 260 pounds
Bats: Left Throws: Left Position: First Base

Regular Season Stats

Year	Team	Games	Hits	HR	RBI	AVG
2004	PHI	19	11	2	5	.282
2005	PHI	88	90	22	63	.288
2006	PHI	159	182	58	149	.313
2007	PHI	144	142	47	136	.268
2008	PHI	162	153	48	146	.251
2009	PHI	160	172	45	141	.279
CAREER		**732**	**750**	**222**	**640**	**.279**

(HR = Home Runs; RBI = Runs Batted In; AVG = Batting Average)

achievements

All-Star selection: 2006
National League MVP: 2006
National League Rookie of the Year: 2005
Led National League in home runs: 2006, 2008
Home Run Derby winner: 2006

fact

Howard is just one of three players to win the Rookie of the Year and MVP awards in back-to-back years.

personal information

Name: Johan Alexander Santana
Born: March 13, 1979, in Tovar, Venezuela
Height: 6 feet
Weight: 210 pounds
Bats: Left   Throws: Left
Position: Starting Pitcher

Regular Season Stats

Year	Team	Games	Wins	Losses	Strikeouts	ERA
2000	MIN	30	2	3	64	6.49
2001	MIN	15	1	0	28	4.74
2002	MIN	27	8	6	137	2.99
2003	MIN	45	12	3	169	3.07
2004	MIN	34	20	6	265	2.61
2005	MIN	33	16	7	238	2.87
2006	MIN	34	19	6	245	2.77
2007	MIN	33	15	13	235	3.33
2008	NYM	34	16	7	206	2.53
2009	NYM	25	13	9	146	3.13
CAREER		**310**	**122**	**60**	**1,733**	**3.12**

(ERA = Earned Run Average)

achievements

All-Star Game selection: 2005, 2006, 2007, 2009
American League Cy Young Award: 2004, 2006
Gold Glove Award: 2007
Led American League in wins (19) in 2006
Won pitching triple crown in 2006 by leading American League in ERA, wins, and strikeouts

fact

Santana started out as a center fielder. He was switched to pitching because of his great arm speed.

Johan Santana

Johan Santana has a blazing fastball and an incredible changeup. His amazing skills have made him one of baseball's best pitchers. Santana started as a relief pitcher for the Minnesota Twins. He soon became a starting pitcher. Santana won the AL Cy Young Award in 2004 and 2006. The lefty was traded to the New York Mets in 2008.

Evan Longoria

Few major leaguers hit the ball like Tampa Bay's Evan Longoria. The third baseman became an instant star in 2008. His sweet swing and great defensive skills made him the 2008 AL Rookie of the Year. He also led the underdog Rays to the playoffs that year. In his first playoff game, he hit two home runs. His great play helped the Rays reach the 2008 World Series.

personal information

Name: Evan Michael Longoria
Born: October 7, 1985, in Downey, California
Height: 6 feet, 2 inches
Weight: 210 pounds
Bats: Right Throws: Right Position: Third Base

Regular Season Stats

Year	Team	Games	Hits	HR	RBI	AVG
2008	TB	122	122	27	85	.272
2009	TB	157	164	33	113	.281
CAREER		**279**	**286**	**60**	**198**	**.277**

(HR = Home Runs; RBI = Runs Batted In; AVG = Batting Average)

achievements

All-Star selection: 2008, 2009
American League Rookie of the Year: 2008
Set Major League rookie record of four home runs in a playoff series in 2008
Represented the United States in the 2009 World Baseball Classic

fact The Tampa Bay Rays made Longoria their first pick (third overall) in the 2006 draft.

Glossary

batting average (BAT-ing AV-uh-rij) — a statistic that measures how often a player gets a base hit; batting average is a player's hit total divided by his total at-bats.

changeup (CHAYNJ-up) — a pitch that is supposed to look like a fastball but is much slower, causing the batter to swing too early

curveball (KURV-bawl) — a pitch that has a lot of spin and changes direction while in the air, which causes the batter to miss

Cy Young Award (SY YUHNG uh-WORD) — the award given to the best pitcher in each league every season; the award honors Hall-of-Fame pitcher Cy Young.

draft (DRAFT) — the process of choosing a person to join a sports organization or team

save (SAYV) — a statistic earned by a relief pitcher for helping his team keep a small lead to win a game

scholarship (SKOL-ur-ship) — a grant or prize that pays for a student to go to college

strikeout (STRIKE-out) — when a pitcher throws three strikes against a batter

strike zone (STRIKE ZOHN) — the area above home plate between the batter's knees and shoulders

Read More

Buckman, Virginia. *Baseball Stars.* Greatest Sports Heroes. New York: Children's Press, 2007.

Doeden, Matt. *The Greatest Baseball Records.* Sports Records. Mankato, Minn.: Capstone Press, 2009.

Edwards, Ethan. *Meet Albert Pujols: Baseball's Power Hitter.* All-Star Players. New York: PowerKids Press, 2009.

Internet Sites

FactHound offers a safe, fun way to find Internet sites related to this book. All of the sites on FactHound have been researched by our staff.

Here's all you do:

Visit *www.facthound.com*

FactHound will fetch the best sites for you!

Index